# Pascal Programming Simple Guide for Beginners

## Understanding the Basic of Pascal Syntax

By

Cohen Barras

# Table of Contents

# CHAPTER 1

# Introduction

## 1.1 What is Pascal

Pascal is a high-level, imperative, and statically typed programming language that was created in the late 1960s by Swiss computer scientist Niklaus Wirth. It was named after the French mathematician and philosopher Blaise Pascal. Pascal was designed with a strong emphasis on readability and structured programming, making it an excellent choice for beginners as well as experienced programmers.

Pascal gained significant popularity in the early days of computing due to its simplicity and efficiency. It was widely used in education and as a development tool for various applications, including scientific and engineering software. One of the most famous Pascal compilers is Turbo Pascal, developed by Borland, which played a significant role in popularizing the language.

Pascal is known for its clean and well-defined syntax, which promotes good coding practices and makes it easier to write bug-free and maintainable code. It also supports strong type-checking, meaning that the data types of variables must be explicitly declared, reducing the chances of type-related errors.

Pascal has evolved over the years, and different dialects of the language have emerged, such as Object Pascal, which introduced object-oriented programming features. Delphi, a popular integrated development environment (IDE), is based on Object Pascal and has been used for developing Windows applications.

## 1.2 Why Learn Pascal

Learning Pascal offers several advantages, even in today's programming landscape, where there are numerous programming languages to choose from:

- **Fundamental Concepts:** Pascal is an excellent language for beginners because it teaches fundamental programming concepts in a straightforward manner. Learning Pascal helps build a solid foundation in programming that can be applied to other languages.

- **Readability:** Pascal's clean and structured syntax encourages good coding practices and enhances code readability. This makes it easier for developers to understand and maintain their programs, which is crucial for collaborative coding and long-term project maintenance.

- **Strong Typing:** Pascal's strong typing system ensures that you explicitly declare variable types, reducing the likelihood of type-related errors. This can lead to more reliable and robust code.

- **Education:** Pascal has historically been used as a teaching language in computer science and programming courses. Learning Pascal can help you grasp core programming concepts before moving on to more complex languages.

- **Legacy Code:** While Pascal may not be as widely used in industry applications as languages like Python, Java, or C++, there is still legacy Pascal code in existence. Understanding Pascal can be valuable if you encounter older systems or have to maintain existing Pascal-based software.

# 1.3 Setting Up Your Pascal Development Environment

Before you start programming in Pascal, you need to set up a development environment. This typically involves installing a Pascal compiler or integrated development environment (IDE) on your computer. Some popular Pascal development tools include Free Pascal, Lazarus (an open-source Pascal IDE), and Dev-Pascal.

Once you've chosen your development environment, you'll need to configure it according to your preferences. This may involve setting up code highlighting, indentation, and other customization options.

Additionally, you may want to install libraries or packages that can extend Pascal's functionality for specific tasks or projects. For example, if you're developing graphical applications, you might need to install graphics libraries compatible with your chosen Pascal environment.

setting up your Pascal development environment is an essential step that allows you to begin writing, testing, and running Pascal programs effectively.

# CHAPTER 2

# Getting Started with Pascal

## 2.1 Your First Pascal Program

Your first Pascal program is the foundation of your journey into Pascal programming. Here are some key points to understand:

- **Program Structure:** Pascal programs are typically structured with specific sections, including the program declaration, uses clause (for including libraries), and the main program block. Understanding this structure is essential to writing your first program.

- **Hello, World!**: The traditional "Hello, World!" program is often the first program beginners write in any programming language.

## 2.2 Variables and Data Types

Variables and data types are fundamental concepts in programming.

- **Variables:** Variables are used to store and manipulate data in a program.

- **Data Types:** Pascal supports various data types, including integers, real numbers, characters, and more. Understanding the differences between these data types and when to use them is crucial for effective programming.

- **Type Safety:** Pascal enforces strict type safety, meaning that variables must be of the correct data type when used. This helps prevent type-related errors and ensures the reliability of your code.

## 2.3 Input and Output in Pascal

Input and output (I/O) are essential for interaction with a program's users and the external world.

- **Displaying Output:** Pascal provides ways to display information to the user, whether it's simple text or more complex data. exploring how to use output functions to present results and messages.

- **User Input:** To make programs interactive, you need to understand how to receive input from users. Pascal allows you to read user input, which can be crucial for creating dynamic applications.

- **Formatted Output:** Sometimes, you'll want to format the output to make it more readable or visually appealing. Pascal provides features for formatting numbers and text.

# CHAPTER 3

# Basic Pascal Syntax

## 3.1 Constants and Variables

- **Constants:** In Pascal, constants are values that do not change during the execution of a program. They can be of various types, such as integer constants, real constants, character constants, and string constants. Constants are often used for values that remain constant throughout the program's execution, like mathematical constants or predefined values.

- **Variables:** Variables, on the other hand, are used to store data that can change during the execution of a program. Variables must be declared with a specific data type, and their values can be modified as the program runs. Pascal enforces strong typing, meaning that you must declare the data type of a variable before using it. This helps catch type-related errors at compile-time rather than runtime.

- **Variable Naming:** When naming variables in Pascal, you should follow naming conventions, which typically include using meaningful names that describe the purpose of the variable. Variable names are case-insensitive in Pascal, which means "myVariable" and "MyVariable" are considered the same variable.

# 3.2 Operators and Expressions

- **Operators:** Pascal supports various operators that allow you to perform operations on constants and variables. These include arithmetic operators (addition, subtraction, multiplication, division), relational operators (equal to, not equal to, less than, greater than), and logical operators (AND, OR, NOT), among others. Understanding how to use these operators is crucial for performing calculations and making decisions in your programs.

- **Expressions:** Expressions in Pascal are combinations of constants, variables, and operators that yield a value. Expressions can be used in assignments, conditions, and other parts of your program. Learning how to create and evaluate expressions is fundamental to performing computations and making your programs functional.

- **Order of Operations:** Just like in mathematics, Pascal follows specific rules for the order of operations when evaluating expressions. Understanding these rules is essential to ensure that your expressions are evaluated correctly.

By grasping the concepts of constants, variables, operators, and expressions in Pascal, equipping to perform various computations and manipulate data within your programs. These foundational elements are essential for building more complex algorithms and applications as you advance in your Pascal programming journey.

## 3.3 Conditional Statements (if-else)

Conditional statements allow your Pascal program to make decisions based on certain conditions. The most common conditional statement is the "if-else" statement.

- **if Statement:** The "if" statement is used to execute a block of code if a specified condition is true. learning how to write conditions using comparison operators (e.g., equal to, greater than) and execute different code blocks based on whether the condition is true or false.

- **else Statement:** The "else" statement is used in conjunction with "if" to specify what code to execute if the condition in the "if" statement is false. This allows your program to take different paths depending on the outcome of the condition.

- **Nested if-else:** nesting "if-else" statements within each other to handle multiple conditions and create more complex decision-making logic.

## 3.4 Loops (while, repeat, for)

Loops are essential for repetitive tasks in programming. Pascal provides several types of loops:

- **while Loop:** The "while" loop repeatedly executes a block of code as long as a specified condition is true. using "while" loops to create loops that continue executing until a certain condition is met.

- **repeat-until Loop:** The "repeat-until" loop is similar to the "while" loop but evaluates the condition after executing the loop's code block. This means the code block always runs at least once before the condition is checked.

- **for Loop:** The "for" loop is used when you know beforehand how many times you want to repeat a certain task. It's often used for iterating over sequences, like arrays or ranges of numbers.

Conditional statements and loops is crucial for controlling the flow of your Pascal programs. These constructs enable you to create programs that can make decisions, perform actions based on conditions, and repeat tasks efficiently. Mastery of these concepts will empower you to create more dynamic and interactive Pascal applications.

# CHAPTER 4

# Procedures and Functions

## 4.1 Defining and Using Procedures

Procedures in Pascal are blocks of code that can be defined and reused throughout your program.

- **Procedure Definition:** understanding how to define a procedure, including specifying its name, parameters, and the code block that it contains. Parameters are variables that allow you to pass data into the procedure for processing.

- **Procedure Call:** learning how to call (invoke) a procedure within your program. When a procedure is called, the program execution jumps to the procedure's code block, executes it, and then returns to the point where the procedure was called.

- **Parameter Passing:** Procedures can receive data through parameters. exploring the different ways to pass data to procedures, including by value and by reference. Understanding how parameter passing works is crucial for effective communication between the calling code and the procedure.

- **Procedure Modularity:** Procedures enhance the

modularity of your code. By breaking down your program into smaller, manageable procedures, you can improve code organization, readability, and maintainability.

## 4.2 Creating Functions

Functions in Pascal are similar to procedures but with one key difference: they return a value.

- **Function Definition:** understanding how to define a function, including specifying its name, parameters, return type, and the code block that calculates and returns a value. Functions are often used to perform calculations or retrieve data and return results to the calling code.

- **Function Call:** Like procedures, learning how to call functions within your program. When a function is called, it executes its code block and returns a value to the calling code.

- **Return Values:** Functions are known for their ability to return values, which can be of various data types. exploring how to use these returned values in your program for further processing or to make decisions.

- **Reusability:** Functions, like procedures, promote code reusability. You can create functions for commonly used calculations or data retrieval tasks and reuse them in multiple parts of your program.

procedures and functions is essential for building modular and maintainable Pascal programs. These constructs allow you to break down complex tasks into manageable pieces of code, making your programs more organized and easier to work with. Additionally, functions provide a way to encapsulate and reuse logic while returning valuable results to the rest of your program.

## 4.3 Scope and Parameters

Understanding scope and parameters is crucial for effectively working with procedures and functions in Pascal:

- **Scope:** Scope refers to the region of a program where a variable or identifier is visible and can be accessed. In Pascal, variables can have different levels of scope:

- **Local Scope:** Variables declared within a procedure or function have local scope, meaning they are only accessible within that specific procedure or function. They are typically used for temporary storage and are not visible outside the procedure or function.

- **Global Scope:** Variables declared outside of any procedure or function have global scope, making them accessible from anywhere in the program. Global variables retain their values across multiple procedure or function calls and can be useful for storing data that needs to be shared among different parts of the program.

- **Parameters:** Parameters are variables that are used to pass data between the calling code and a procedure or function. Parameters are defined within the parentheses of the procedure or function declaration and serve as placeholders for data that will be passed when the procedure or function is called.

- **Formal Parameters:** These are the parameters declared in the procedure or function header. They specify the data type and name of the parameter that will be used within the procedure or function. Formal parameters are variables local to the procedure or function.

- **Actual Parameters (Arguments):** These are the values or variables that are provided when calling a procedure or function. They are passed to the formal parameters defined in the procedure or function declaration. The actual parameters can be constants, variables, or expressions.

- **Passing Parameters:** Pascal allows parameters to be passed by value or by reference. Understanding the difference is crucial:

- **Pass by Value:** When a parameter is passed by value, a copy of the parameter's value is sent to the procedure or function. Any changes made to the parameter within the procedure or function do not affect the original value outside of it.

- **Pass by Reference:** When a parameter is passed by reference, the procedure or function operates directly on the original variable. Any modifications to the parameter within the procedure or function will affect the original variable outside of it.

- **Parameter Scope:** Parameters, whether formal or actual, have their own scope within the procedure or function. This means that the names of parameters can be the same as names of global variables or other parameters within the procedure or function without causing conflicts.

scope and parameters is fundamental for writing modular and maintainable Pascal code. Properly managing scope ensures that variables are used in the intended context and prevents unintended side effects. Skillful use of parameters allows you to pass data seamlessly between different parts of your program, enhancing code reusability and flexibility.

# CHAPTER 5

# Arrays and Records

## 5.1 Working with Arrays

- **Arrays:** An array is a collection of elements of the same data type, organized in a contiguous memory block. Arrays are useful when you need to work with a group of related data items. In Pascal, arrays can be one-dimensional, two-dimensional, or even multi-dimensional.

- **Array Declaration:** learning how to declare an array, specifying its data type, name, and size. For example, you can declare an integer array to store a list of numbers.

- **Accessing Array Elements:** Arrays are accessed using indices, which indicate the position of an element within the array. Pascal uses zero-based indexing, meaning the first element has an index of 0, the second element has an index of 1, and so on.

- **Array Operations:** exploring various operations you can perform on arrays, such as initializing an array, assigning values to its elements, and reading values from it.

- **Array Length:** Unlike some modern programming languages, Pascal does not provide a built-in mechanism to automatically determine the length of an array. Therefore, you'll need to keep track of the array's length yourself.

# 5.2 Introduction to Records

- **Records:** Records, also known as structures or structs in other programming languages, allow you to define custom data types that can hold multiple fields of different data types. Each field in a record is called a member or field.

- **Record Declaration:** learning how to declare a record by specifying its name and defining its fields. Fields can have different data types, such as integers, strings, or other records.

- **Accessing Record Fields:** To access the data stored in a record, you use dot notation, specifying the record variable followed by the field name. This allows you to read and modify the individual components of a record.

- **Custom Data Structures:** Records are useful for creating custom data structures to represent complex entities in your program. For example, you might use a record to represent a student with fields like name, ID, and GPA.

- **Passing Records as Parameters:** Records can be passed as parameters to procedures or functions, allowing you to work with structured data in your program. This is especially useful when you need to pass multiple pieces of information together.

Working with arrays and records in Pascal is essential for managing and organizing data in your programs. Arrays are suitable for working with collections of similar data, while records provide a way to create custom data structures to represent more complex entities. Understanding how to declare, access, and manipulate these data structures is crucial for effective Pascal programming.

# 5.3 Combining Arrays and Records

Combining arrays and records in Pascal allows you to create complex data structures that store and manage structured data efficiently. Here's an overview of how you can combine these two concepts:

- **Arrays of Records:** One common way to combine arrays and records is by creating arrays where each element is a record. For example, you might have an array of records to represent a list of students, where each record stores information like name, ID, and GPA. This combination allows you to organize and manage structured data effectively.

- **Multi-Dimensional Arrays of Records:** You can extend the concept further by creating multi-dimensional arrays of records. For instance, you might have a two-dimensional array of records to represent a grid of data, such as a spreadsheet with rows and columns. Each element of the array would then be a record containing information relevant to a cell in the grid.

- **Nested Records:** Another way to combine arrays and records is by using nested records. This means that a record can contain fields that are themselves arrays or records. For example, you might have a record to represent a department in a university, and one of its fields could be an array of student records. This allows you to create hierarchical data structures.

- **Searching and Sorting:** Combining arrays of records allows you to perform operations like searching and sorting efficiently. You can search for records based on specific criteria (e.g., finding all students with a GPA above a certain threshold) and sort records based on one or more fields (e.g., sorting students by name or GPA).

- **Data Organization:** Combining arrays and records is essential for organizing and managing structured data in your Pascal programs. It helps you represent real-world entities and relationships in a way that's both intuitive and efficient.

- **Modularity:** Using arrays of records or nested records promotes modularity in your code. You can create procedures or functions that operate on these data structures, making your code more organized and easier to maintain.

- **Data Validation:** With records, you can enforce data validation rules by encapsulating related fields within a record. This ensures that data remains consistent and accurate within your program.

By combining arrays and records in Pascal, you can create powerful data structures that enable you to model and manipulate complex data effectively. Whether you're building a database, managing student records, or handling any structured data, this combination provides you with the tools to do so efficiently and intuitively.

# CHAPTER 6

# File Handling in Pascal

## 6.1 Reading and Writing Files

- **File Handling in Pascal:** File handling allows your Pascal programs to interact with external files on your computer's storage. This interaction includes reading data from files and writing data to them. Files can be used for various purposes, such as data storage, configuration settings, or working with large datasets.

- **File Types:** In Pascal, you can work with various types of files, including text files and binary files. Each type has its specific use cases and characteristics.

- **Opening and Closing Files:** Before you can read from or write to a file, you must open it using the **File** data type and specific file handling procedures or functions. After performing the necessary operations, you should close the file to free up system resources.

- **Reading from Files:** Reading from files involves techniques to retrieve data from external files and store it in your program's variables. Pascal provides file handling procedures and functions for reading lines, characters, or entire records from files.

- **Writing to Files:** Writing to files allows you to save data generated by your program to external files. You can write individual items, such as numbers or text, or entire data structures like records or arrays to files.

# 6.2 Text and Binary Files

- **Text Files:** Text files are files that store data as human-readable text. They consist of characters, including letters, digits, symbols, and whitespace. Text files are commonly used for storing configuration files, logs, and data that is intended to be readable by both humans and computers. Reading and writing text files in Pascal typically involve procedures like **Readln** and **Writeln**.

- **Binary Files:** Binary files, on the other hand, store data in a binary format, which means the data is represented as sequences of bytes. Binary files are used for various purposes, including storing program data structures, images, audio, or any data that doesn't need to be human-readable. Reading and writing binary files in Pascal involves procedures like **BlockRead** and **BlockWrite**.

- **Data Serialization:** When working with binary files, it's often necessary to serialize and deserialize data. Serialization is the process of converting data structures (such as records or objects) into a binary format that can be written to a file. Deserialization is the reverse process of reading the binary data from a file and reconstructing the original data structure.

- **Considerations:** When choosing between text and binary files, consider factors such as the type of data you're working with, file size, data integrity, and the need for human readability. Text files are easier for humans to inspect, while binary files are more efficient for storing complex data structures or large datasets.

file handling in Pascal, including reading and writing text and binary files, is essential for working with external data sources, managing persistent data storage, and interacting with files in various applications. It allows your programs to read data from files, update existing files, and create new ones, expanding the range of tasks you can accomplish with your Pascal applications.

# CHAPTER 7

# Advanced Pascal Concepts

## 7.1 Pointers and Memory Management

- **Pointers:** Pointers are variables that store memory addresses. They allow you to indirectly access and manipulate data stored in memory. In Pascal, pointers are declared using the ^ symbol, and they can point to data of various types, including integers, records, and other pointers.

- **Dynamic Memory Allocation:** One of the key uses of pointers in Pascal is for dynamic memory allocation. Unlike statically allocated memory (e.g., variables with fixed sizes), dynamic memory allocation allows you to allocate and deallocate memory at runtime. This is particularly useful when you need to work with data structures of unknown or varying sizes.

- **New and Dispose:** In Pascal, you use the **New** operator to allocate memory dynamically for a data structure, and the **Dispose** procedure to release (free) the allocated memory when it's no longer needed. Proper memory management is crucial to prevent memory leaks and ensure efficient use of system resources.

- **Common Pointer Operations:**
  You can perform various
  operations with pointers,
  including dereferencing
  (accessing the data pointed to
  by a pointer), assigning
  pointers, and using pointer
  arithmetic (e.g., incrementing
  or decrementing a pointer to
  access adjacent memory
  locations).

- **Heap and Stack:** In Pascal,
  memory is typically divided
  into two main regions: the stack
  and the heap. The stack is used
  for storing local variables and
  function call information, while
  the heap is used for dynamic
  memory allocation.
  Understanding the distinction
  between these two memory

regions is vital for efficient memory management.

- **Memory Safety:** While pointers provide powerful capabilities, they also introduce potential issues, such as null pointer dereferencing and memory leaks. It's essential to follow best practices in pointer usage to ensure memory safety and avoid crashes or unexpected behavior.

- **Applications:** Pointers are commonly used in advanced Pascal programming scenarios, such as building data structures like linked lists, trees, and graphs, as well as interfacing with external libraries and performing low-level memory manipulation.

- **Type Safety:** Pascal is known for its strong type system, which extends to pointers. When declaring and using pointers, you must ensure that the pointer's data type matches the type of data it points to. This type safety helps prevent type-related errors and enhances program reliability.

- **Pointer to Functions:** In Pascal, you can also use pointers to functions, allowing you to call functions indirectly through a pointer. This feature is often used in advanced scenarios, such as creating function tables or implementing callback mechanisms.

pointers and memory management is an advanced topic in Pascal and is typically reserved for situations where fine-grained control over memory allocation and data manipulation is required. While powerful, it comes with a responsibility to manage memory properly to avoid memory leaks and other memory-related issues.

## 7.2 Object-Oriented Programming in Pascal

- **Object-Oriented Programming (OOP):** Object-Oriented Programming is a programming paradigm that organizes code into objects, each of which represents an instance of a class. OOP promotes the principles of encapsulation, inheritance, and polymorphism, allowing for modular and organized code design.

- **Classes and Objects:** In Pascal, classes are used to define blueprints for objects, while objects are instances of these classes. A class defines the properties (attributes) and behaviors (methods) that objects of that class will have.

- **Encapsulation:** Encapsulation is the principle of bundling data (attributes) and the methods (functions or procedures) that operate on that data into a single unit, i.e., a class. This helps hide the internal details of an object and exposes only the necessary functionality to the outside world.

- **Inheritance:** Inheritance is a mechanism that allows you to create new classes (subclasses or derived classes) based on existing classes (base classes or parent classes). Subclasses inherit the properties and behaviors of their parent classes and can extend or override them.

- **Polymorphism:** Polymorphism allows different objects to respond to the same method or function call in a way that is appropriate for their specific class. This enables code to be more flexible and adaptable to different object types.

- **Method Overriding:** In OOP, you can override (replace) a method defined in a base class with a new implementation in a derived class. This allows you to provide specialized behavior for specific object types.

- **Abstract Classes and Interfaces:** Pascal supports abstract classes, which are classes that cannot be instantiated directly but serve as base classes for other classes. Interfaces define a contract that classes must implement, ensuring that certain methods are available.

- **Access Control:** Pascal provides access control modifiers like **private**, **protected**, and **public**, which determine the visibility of class members (attributes and methods). This helps maintain encapsulation and controls which parts of a class are accessible from outside.

- **Object Creation and Destruction:** In OOP, you create objects by instantiating classes, and objects can be destroyed when they are no longer needed. Pascal provides mechanisms for creating and destroying objects, often involving constructors and destructors.

- **Object-Oriented Design Patterns:** OOP in Pascal often involves the application of design patterns, which are reusable solutions to common software design problems. Examples include the Singleton pattern, Factory pattern, and Observer pattern.

- **Examples:** Object-oriented programming in Pascal can be applied to various domains, including software development, game development, graphical user interfaces (GUIs), and database applications.

Object-Oriented Programming in Pascal allows for the creation of structured, maintainable, and extensible code. It is particularly useful for modeling real-world entities and relationships in software applications, making it easier to manage complexity and improve code reusability. By defining classes and using objects, you can create modular and organized code that can be adapted and extended as your software requirements evolve.

# CHAPTER 8

# Error Handling and Debugging

## 8.1 Common Programming Errors

- **Syntax Errors:** Syntax errors are among the most common types of errors in programming. They occur when your Pascal code does not conform to the language's syntax rules. Examples include missing semicolons at the end of statements, unmatched parentheses, or using reserved keywords as identifiers.

- **Type Errors:** Type errors occur when you attempt to use a variable or value of one data type in a way that is not compatible with another data type. For instance, trying to add a string to an integer or comparing values of different data types can lead to type errors.

- **Logical Errors:** Logical errors, also known as semantic errors, are more challenging to detect than syntax errors. They occur when the program's logic is incorrect, leading to undesired or unexpected behavior. Debugging logical errors often involves careful inspection of your code's logic and algorithms.

- **Runtime Errors:** Runtime errors occur when a program is executing and encounters an issue that cannot be determined until runtime. Common examples include division by zero, array index out of bounds, and attempting to access a null pointer.

- **Null Reference Errors:** In Pascal, when you work with pointers, you need to be cautious about null (nil) references. Accessing a nil pointer can result in a runtime error and program termination. Properly initializing and checking pointers is crucial to avoid null reference errors.

- **Array Index Errors:** Using incorrect array indices can lead to array index errors. For instance, attempting to access an element beyond the bounds of an array can result in an "array index out of bounds" error. Properly validating array indices and bounds is essential.

- **Resource Leaks:** In Pascal, when working with files, memory allocation, or other resources, failing to release (dispose of) those resources properly can lead to resource leaks. Resource leaks can cause your program to consume excessive memory or fail to close files, which can lead to data corruption.

- **Infinite Loops:** Writing loops that do not have proper termination conditions can result in infinite loops, causing your program to hang or become unresponsive. Always ensure that loops have exit conditions.

- **Division by Zero:** Division by zero is a common runtime error that occurs when you attempt to divide a number by zero. To avoid this error, make sure you check for zero denominators before performing division operations.

- **Uninitialized Variables:** Accessing the value of an uninitialized variable can lead to unpredictable behavior and bugs. Always initialize your variables before using them to avoid this issue.

- **Overflows:** Pascal has limits on the range of numeric data types. Performing calculations that result in values exceeding these limits can lead to overflow errors. Properly handle numeric data and check for potential overflows.

- **Exception Handling:** In Pascal, you can use exception handling mechanisms to gracefully handle errors and exceptions. Catching and handling exceptions allows you to provide more informative error messages and recover from unexpected issues.

Identifying and fixing common programming errors is an integral part of software development. Debugging tools and practices, such as using IDEs (Integrated Development Environments), code analysis tools, and step-by-step code execution, can help you locate and correct these errors effectively.

## 8.2 Debugging Techniques

Debugging is an essential skill in programming, and Pascal provides various debugging techniques to help you identify and resolve issues in your code. Here are some debugging techniques commonly used in Pascal:

- **Print Statements:** One of the simplest debugging techniques is to insert print statements (e.g., **WriteLn**) in your code to display variable values and the program's flow. This can help you understand how your program behaves at different points and identify issues.

- **IDE Debugging Tools:** Integrated Development Environments (IDEs) like Lazarus or Delphi come with built-in debugging tools. These tools allow you to set breakpoints, step through code, inspect variables, and watch the program's execution in real-time.

- **Breakpoints:** Breakpoints are markers you can set in your code, typically at lines where you suspect issues might occur. When the program reaches a breakpoint during execution, it pauses, allowing you to inspect variables and step through the code.

- **Step Through Code:** Debuggers in IDEs often provide options to step through your code one line at a time. You can step into functions or procedures, step over lines, or step out of functions to trace the program's execution path.

- **Inspect Variables:** Debuggers allow you to inspect the values of variables at runtime. This can help you identify incorrect values or understand how variables change as the program runs.

- **Call Stack:** Debuggers often display the call stack, which shows the sequence of function and procedure calls leading up to the current point in the code. This can be invaluable for understanding the program's flow and identifying issues related to function calls.

- **Watch Expressions:** You can set up watch expressions in debuggers to monitor specific variables or expressions. The debugger will update the values of these expressions as you step through the code.

- **Conditional Breakpoints:** Some debuggers allow you to set conditional breakpoints, which break execution only if a specified condition is met. This is useful for focusing on specific scenarios or edge cases.

- **Profiling Tools:** Profiling tools can help you identify performance bottlenecks and memory usage issues. They provide insights into which parts of your code consume the most resources.

- **Code Reviews:** Sometimes, a fresh pair of eyes can spot issues you might have missed. Conducting code reviews with colleagues or peers can be an effective debugging technique.

- **Unit Testing:** Writing unit tests for your code can help you catch issues early in the development process. Automated tests can verify that your functions and procedures produce the expected results.

- **Version Control:** Version control systems like Git allow you to track changes in your codebase. You can use version control to revert to previous versions if you encounter issues, helping you identify when problems were introduced.

- **Error Messages:** Pay attention to error messages and exceptions. They often provide valuable information about what went wrong. Use these messages as starting points for debugging.

- **Documentation and Documentation Comments:** Well-documented code and documentation comments (e.g., using PascalDoc or Doxygen syntax) can make it easier to understand code behavior and logic, aiding in debugging efforts.

Effective debugging involves a combination of these techniques, depending on the nature of the problem and your development environment. Developing good debugging skills is an ongoing process, and with practice, you'll become more proficient at identifying and resolving issues in your Pascal code.